Save the Sea Turtles!

Written by Alice Leonhardt

STECK-VAUGHN
ELEMENTARY · SECONDARY · ADULT · LIBRARY

A Harcourt Classroom Education Company

www.steck-vaughn.com

What animal is as old as the dinosaurs?

The sea turtle is!

Sea turtles have been on Earth for millions of years.

Today we do not have dinosaurs.

But we do have sea turtles.

3

Sea turtles live in oceans all over the world.

Most of them like warm salt water.

They have powerful flippers for swimming.

They paddle with their strong front flippers.

Their back flippers help them turn and stop.

Some sea turtles can swim twenty miles an hour!

Sea turtles are different from land turtles.

A sea turtle's shell is softer than a land turtle's shell.

The soft shell helps the sea turtle swim.

A sea turtle also can't pull its head into its shell.

It has something else to protect itself.

It has thick skin on its neck and head.

Sea turtles can see far away under water.

This helps them hunt for food.

Sometimes sea turtles look like they are crying.

They are really getting rid of salt.

Sea turtles take in a lot of salt from the water.

They get rid of the extra salt in their tears.

Sea turtles are endangered.

That means that not many are alive.

Some people hunt sea turtles for food.

They use the shells to make jewelry.

Sea turtles also get caught in fishing nets.

Trapped turtles drown if they cannot get air.

Female sea turtles lay their eggs on sandy beaches.

Today there are fewer beaches for nesting.

People build roads and walls along some beaches.

They build hotels and houses.

Sea turtles do not like the lights and the noise.

They will not come to these beaches to lay their eggs.

Many people are helping sea turtles.

Some fishermen use nets that let the turtles swim out.

Other people try to protect the beaches.

They want quiet places for sea turtles to lay eggs.

People have made laws, too.

The laws keep sea turtles from being killed.

What can you do to help the sea turtles?
If you see sea turtles, do not scare them.
Do not touch their eggs or dig up their nests.
If you help, sea turtles may live on Earth
for many more years.